The Best Of QED COOKS

with Chris Fennimore
© 2001 WQED Pittsburgh VOL. 2

Produced by WQED Pittsburgh, 4802 Fifth Ave.,
Pittsburgh, PA 15213; 412/622-1300; www.wqed.org.

Recipe compilation:
Chris Fennimore

Project manager/editor:
Michelle Pilecki

Cookbook designer:
Audrey Galata

Production Manager:
Julie Lewis

Photography:
Blaine Stiger

Project editors:
Mike May, Dana Black
Joyce DeFrancesco

Sales director:
Rick Vaccarelli

Vice president publishing
and Internet services:
Chris Fletcher

WQED Pittsburgh
creative director:
Michael Maskarinec

*recipes
in italics
illustrated*

Table of Contents

Who We Are

For more than 45 years, WQED Pittsburgh has been the region's electronic equivalent of the concert hall, the theater and the public library. Through public television, all-classical FM radio, the Internet, a nationally recognized award-winning regional magazine and the WQED Learning Center, WQED has provided drama, ballet, music, art, architecture, public affairs, education and history to virtually every household in Western Pennsylvania, plus many more across the border in Ohio, West Virginia and Maryland.

STATION WQED

Television station, located here, opened April 1954, as first community-sponsored educational television station in America. In 1955 it was the first to telecast classes to elementary schools.

PENNSYLVANIA HISTORICAL AND MUSEUM COMMISSION

WQED PITTSBURGH is WQED 13, WQED-FM 89.3/WQEJ-FM 89.7 Johnstown, PITTSBURGH magazine and www.wqed.org, but the organization is more than what you see or hear over the airwaves. WQED brings its resources into the community in a variety of ways—through special projects and local programming, including the nightly "On Q magazine." We also develop and implement regional teacher training, promote diverse local arts/cultural organizations, oversee distribution partnerships, and develop an increasing array of interactive and multimedia products for local and national audiences.

FOUNDED IN 1954, WQED was the country's first community-owned television station. Later it became a production center for national programs for the Public Broadcasting Service (PBS). The organization has distinguished itself by its original programming both locally and nationally, and has been recognized with more than 250 regional, national and international awards for excellence, including 64 Emmy and 12 Peabody awards. ➤ ➤ ➤

Membership

It's time to get cookin' with WQED Pittsburgh. Membership definitely has its privileges.

Get any of the "QED Cooks" cookbooks (see list on page 7) for a $60 pledge of support, including Chris Fennimore's latest books, *"B" Is for Brunch, "C" Is for Chili* and *"I" Is for Italian*. Get two books of your choice for $100, or three for $130.

Pledge $350 to WQED and get a baker's dozen of "QED Cooks" cookbooks. Or get the complete set of cookbooks for $700.

And remember, any pledge of $40 or more entitles you to membership in WQED.

Here are just a few of the perks: ➤ ➤ ➤

$40 Basic Membership:
- 12 issues of award-winning PITTSBURGH magazine
- WQED Membercard with valuable discounts for members only

$50 Family Membership:
- All items at the Basic Membership level plus
- Invitation to WQED Pittsburgh's annual Open House

$250-$999 Producers Society:
- All items at the Family Membership level plus
- Invitations to special events and screenings
- The ability to purchase WQED thank-you gifts at special Producers Society prices

$1,000 and above Leadership Circle:
- All items at the Producers Society level plus
- Invitations to exclusive receptions
- Unlimited use of the video lending library

$1,000 and above FM Angels:
- All items at the Basic Membership level plus

- The chance to be a guest announcer on WQED-FM
- Invitations to special WQED-FM events with visiting classical-music performers and your favorite on-air hosts

$50 and $250 Jukebox Club:
- All items at the Basic Membership level plus
- Quarterly WQED Jukebox Club newsletter
- Advance opportunity for tickets to special doo-wop concerts and events

For more information on becoming a member of WQED, call the membership hotline at 412/622-1370; toll-free 800/876-1316; or www.wqed.org.

If you'd like to volunteer to answer phones during our membership drives, help us during community events or learn more about volunteer opportunities at WQED 13 and WQED-FM, call 412/622-1590.

QED Cooks Cookbooks

"A" Is for Appetizers
"B" Is for Berries
"B" Is for Bread
"B" Is for Brunch
Best of QED Cooks Vol. 1
"C" Is for Candy
"C" Is for Casseroles
   and Covered Dishes
"C" Is for Cookie
"C" Is for Chicken

"C" Is for Chili
Church Lady Cooking
"D" Is for Desserts
"E" Is for Ethnic
Firehouse Cooking
Food for Cold Winter Days
Food for Warm Summer Days
"G" Is for Gifts
"H" Is for Harvest
"H" Is for Healthy

"I" Is for Italian
"K" Is for Kids in the Kitchen
"M" Is for Meat
"M" Is for Mom
"P" Is for Pasta
"P" Is for Pie
"P" Is for Potato
Pittsburgh Celebrities Cook
"Q" Is for Quick and Easy
"S" Is for Salads

"S" Is for Seafood
"S" Is for Soups
   and Stews
"S" Is for Sunday Dinners
Soup to Nuts
"T" Is for Tailgate
"T" Is for Tomato
"V" Is for Vegetable
"Z" Is for Zucchini

Appetizers and Snacks

We had a cooking marathon devoted specifically to appetizers in 1994. More recently, we had a windfall of snack recipes when we did " 'T' Is for Tailgating" in the fall of 1999. Appetizers are often among the most interesting and tasty items on a menu. It's fun to have a potluck get-together with friends, where everyone brings appetizers. These recipes are also great for picnics and tailgating, when you want to have foods that are easy to handle and don't necessarily need to be served hot.

Stuffed Cherry Tomatoes

INGREDIENTS

60 cherry tomatoes

12 walnut halves

1 lb. cream cheese

5 oz. gorgonzola cheese

1 Tbs. cognac

Salt and fresh ground pepper

Fresh chives, finely chopped

1 Tbs. savory

DIRECTIONS

Cup a small cap from the top of each tomato. With a small spoon, scoop out the flesh. Invert the tomatoes on a plate to drain.

Grate the walnuts and set aside. Combine white and blue cheese in a dish and mash them together with a fork, incorporating the cognac and a little salt and pepper, or process the cheeses in a food processor. When the mixture is smooth, add the walnuts, chives and savory. Mix again until well-blended.

Pipe or spoon mixture into the tomato shells.

SERVING
60 appetizers

NOTES
This recipe might be the inspiration for you to start a window-box herb garden. For small amounts of basil, chives, oregano, etc. there's nothing like snipping a few leaves from your own plants—and it's much cheaper.

SUBMITTED BY:
Susan Mihalo Van Riper

Panther Paws

INGREDIENTS

1 lb. ground beef

1 lb. hot Italian sausage (use
bulk or remove casings)

1 lb. Velveeta cheese, cut up

1 tsp. oregano

1 tsp. garlic powder

1 tsp. Worcestershire sauce

2 loaves party rye bread

DIRECTIONS

Brown the meats together in a nonstick skillet. Drain thoroughly. Combine the cheese with the meats until the cheese is melted. Add the spices and incorporate thoroughly.

Cover a cookie sheet with plastic wrap or freezer wrap. Spread 1 tablespoon of the mixture on each bread slice, place in a single layer on the cookie sheet, and freeze. When frozen, seal the "paws" in plastic bags.

Keep frozen until the Pittsburgh Panthers play. Bake frozen on a cookie sheet at 350° for 15 minutes. Hail to Pitt!

SERVING

Makes about 4 dozen

NOTES

If your gang prefers a Mexican twist, use chili powder instead of the garlic and oregano, and about 1/2 cup of salsa instead of the Worcestershire sauce.

SUBMITTED BY:
Daniel K. Boyd

Ham and Cheese Pie

INGREDIENTS

For the filling

2 c. creamed cottage cheese

2 c. ricotta cheese

2 c cooked ham, diced

2/3 c. parmesan cheese, grated

3 eggs

2 tsp. Italian seasoning

1/2 tsp. salt

1/4 tsp. pepper

For the pastry

Pastry for two-crust 9-inch pie
   (your own or store-bought)

1 egg yolk, beaten

DIRECTIONS

For the filling

In a medium bowl, mix the cheeses, ham, eggs and seasonings. Set aside.

Prepare pastry

With hands, shape two-thirds of the pastry into a large ball. Shape remaining dough into another ball. On lightly floured surface with floured rolling pin, roll large ball into a 16-inch circle, about 1/8-inch thick. Fold circle into fourths and carefully line into a 10-inch spring-form pan. Unfold. With fingers, lightly press pastry into the bottom and sides of the pan. Trim edges of pastry to make it even with the rim of pan. Brush pastry all over with some beaten egg yolk.

Spoon cheese mixture into pastry-lined pan. Fold edges of pastry over filling. Brush pastry with some beaten egg yolk. Preheat oven to 375°.

Fold remaining pastry ball into a 10-inch circle. With knife or pastry-cutter, cut design in pastry. Place pastry circle over filling in pan, press lightly around edges to seal. Brush top with remaining egg yolk.

Bake 1 hour or until knife inserted in center comes out clean. Cool pie in refrigerator until serving time.

To serve: Carefully remove sides of springform pan. With sharp knife, cut pie into moderately thick slices.

SERVING

Makes 12-14 appetizer slices

NOTES

I have substituted cooked Italian sausage, a mix of ham and prosciutto, and portobello and shiitake mushrooms for ham. I have added to the original recipe sun-dried tomatoes, portobello mushrooms, lightly steamed broccoli, chives and shallots.

SUBMITTED BY:
Susan Mihalo VanRiper

Mozzarella and Ham Kebabs

INGREDIENTS

2 Tbs. olive oil

1/2 tsp. salt

1/4 tsp. pepper

1/2 tsp. oregano

1/4 tsp. dried basil

1/4 tsp. crushed red pepper

5 fresh mozzarella balls

5 thin slices of prosciutto

1 (7 1/2-oz.) jar roasted
   red peppers

Fresh basil leaves or
   Italian parsley

DIRECTIONS

Mix together the oil and spices. Cut the mozzarella balls into small cubes (about 1/2 inch) and marinate in the spiced oil mixture one hour or overnight. Cut prosciutto into small pieces (about an inch).

Thread the pepper, cheese, basil and prosciutto onto toothpicks. Repeat until all ingredients are used.

SERVING
Makes about 4 dozen

NOTES
Fresh mozzarella has a much different flavor and texture from the shrink-wrapped packages you may be accustomed to grating for pizza. The fresh has a light taste and absorbs the flavors of the spices in which it is marinated.

SUBMITTED BY:
Barbara Knezovich

Caponata

INGREDIENTS

3/4 c. olive oil

1 large eggplant, cut into
bite-sized pieces

6 medium zucchini, cut into
bite-sized pieces

1/2 lb. mushrooms, thickly sliced

1 1/2 c. chopped onions

1 c. sliced celery

1 garlic clove, crushed

1/2 c. red wine vinegar

1/4 c. capers, drained

2 Tbs. sugar

1 tsp. salt

1/4 tsp. pepper

3 large tomatoes, cut into
bite-sized pieces

1 (4 1/2-oz.) jar pimento-stuffed
olives, halved crosswise

DIRECTIONS

In 8-quart dutch oven or large saucepot over high heat, in hot olive oil, cook eggplant, zucchini, mushrooms, onions, celery and garlic for 10 minutes, stirring occasionally. Stir in vinegar, capers, sugar, salt and pepper. Reduce heat to low. Cover and simmer 5-10 minutes until vegetables are fork-tender. Stir in tomato chunks and the halved olives. Over high heat, heat to boiling.

Spoon vegetables into large bowl. Cover and refrigerate at least 3 hours or until mixture is chilled. Serve with pita wedges or slices of roasted lamb.

This is also great as a first course or as an accompaniment for cold, sliced meats.

SERVING
8-10

NOTES
This also serves as a delicious sauce for penne pasta. Just heat it in a large skillet and add the cooked macaroni. Stir for a few minutes until the pasta is well-coated, and serve with lots of grated romano cheese.

SUBMITTED BY:
Susan Mihalo VanRiper

Roasted Eggplant Pistounade

SERVING
8-10

NOTES
Make sure you don't
puree this into a paste.
Part of the unique flavor of
this dish is the slightly
chunky texture.

SUBMITTED BY:
Joseph Certo

INGREDIENTS

2 large eggplants

3/4 c. imported green olives

1 roasted red pepper

1 15-oz. can drained
    chickpeas

1/4 c. fruity olive oil

2 Tbs. fresh lemon juice

2 Tbs. drained capers

1/2 c. reconstituted sun-dried
    slivered tomato halves

1/4 c. minced fresh parsley

1/4 c. slivered fresh basil

Salt and pepper to taste

About 24 toasted rounds
    of French bread

DIRECTIONS

Preheat oven to 400°. Line a roasting pan with aluminum foil. Rub eggplants with a little olive oil. Prick the eggplants in several places. Bake 45-50 minutes, turning occasionally. Let cool. Halve eggplants. Scoop out pulp and place into mixing bowl.

While the eggplants are roasting, pit and coarsely chop the green olives. Seed and coarsely chop the red pepper. Place olives, red pepper and chickpeas into food processor. Pulse briefly to make a coarsely chopped mixture, not a puree. Add the 1/4 cup olive oil and lemon juice. Pulse again. Stir chickpea mixture into the eggplant pulp. Add capers, tomatoes, parsley and basil. Stir. Season with salt and pepper. Transfer pistounade to a decorative bowl or crock. Cover and refrigerate for 1 hour.

Serve at room temperature on French bread rounds.

Lemon-Marinated Mushrooms

INGREDIENTS

3/4 c. salad oil

1/4 c. olive oil

1/2 c. lemon juice

1 medium onion, chopped fine

1 tsp. salt

1/4 tsp. pepper

3 bay leaves

1 tsp. chopped parsley

11/2 c. fresh tiny mushrooms or
   3 (4-oz.) cans button
   mushrooms

DIRECTIONS

Place all ingredients except mushrooms into a jar with a screw top. Shake well. Add mushrooms. Shake gently to cover the mushrooms.

Let stand, refrigerated, 12 hours or more.

SERVING
Makes 1 pint

NOTES
Try to find a jar that just fits the mushrooms. When you add the marinade, it should completely cover the mushrooms.

SUBMITTED BY:
Stephanie Matiak

Tortilla Wrap-Ups

SERVING
Makes 120

NOTES

For an interesting variation, spread the tortilla with Russian dressing, sprinkle with drained sauerkraut, and use slices of corned beef and swiss cheese. Bake them in the oven for a few minutes, until the cheese melts, and serve warm.

SUBMITTED BY:
Jan Herrle

INGREDIENTS

12 large flour tortillas

8 oz. bacon/horseradish sour cream dip

12 romaine lettuce leaves

1/2 lb. sliced roast beef or corned beef

DIRECTIONS

Layer each tortilla with the sour cream dip, a lettuce leaf and thin slices of roast or corned beef. Roll up the tortilla and secure with a toothpick.

Refrigerate 1 hour or more. Just before serving, slice into pinwheels and arrange on a platter or tray.

Deviled Almonds

INGREDIENTS

1 1/2 c. blanched whole almonds

1/4 c. margarine

1/4 c. salad oil

1 Tbs. celery salt

1/2 tsp. salt

1/2 tsp. chili powder

1/8 tsp. cayenne

DIRECTIONS

In a heavy skillet, combine almonds, margarine and salad oil. Cook and stir over medium heat until almonds are golden-brown.

Remove almonds and drain on paper towels.

Combine celery salt, salt, chili powder and cayenne. Sprinkle over hot almonds and stir to coat completely.

SERVING
Makes 1 1/2 cups

NOTES
The big problem is making enough of these so that there are some left when company arrives. Better make a double batch.

SUBMITTED BY:
Lola Olinski

Chocolate Truffles

INGREDIENTS

10 oz. semisweet chocolate,
  cut into small pieces

3/4 c. heavy cream

4 Tbs. unsalted butter,
  cut into small pieces

SERVING
Makes 24

NOTES
Use your imagination
to create different flavors
of truffles: orange,
lemon, walnut, even
tarragon truffles.

SUBMITTED BY:
Jim Baran

DIRECTIONS

Melt chocolate and cream in a double boiler until mixture is smooth. Stir in butter until mixture is smooth. Refrigerate until firm. Roll mixture into 1-inch balls. Roll in cocoa powder or confectioners' sugar to coat.

Refrigerate until ready to serve.

Variations:

Raspberry Truffles: After adding butter, add 1/2 cup seedless raspberry jam and 2 tablespoons raspberry brandy or liqueur (such as Chambord). Stir until well-blended. Proceed as above.

Espresso Truffles: After adding butter, add 1 tablespoon instant espresso powder. Stir until well-blended. Proceed as above.

Chocolate Mint Truffles: After adding butter, add 1 1/2 tablespoons finely minced fresh mint. Stir until well-blended. Proceed as above.

Ginger Dip with Apples and Pears

INGREDIENTS

1 (8-oz.) package softened
  cream cheese

1 c. plain yogurt

1/4 c. honey

2 Tbs. grated fresh ginger root

1 8 oz. can crushed pineapple,
  drained

1 Tbs. ascorbic acid mixture

1/3 c. water

2 pears, cored and sliced

2 red apples, cored and sliced

1 golden apple, cored and sliced

1 Tbs. finely chopped almonds

DIRECTIONS

Beat cream cheese, yogurt, honey and ginger until creamy. Fold in the pineapple. Cover and refrigerate to blend the flavors, about 1 hour.

Mix the ascorbic acid mixture and water. Dip the sliced fruit into the mixture to prevent darkening and drain. Just before serving, sprinkle the dip with the almonds. Serve with fruit.

SERVING
4

NOTES
The ascorbic acid mixture is available in most supermarkets, usually near the baking soda. If you can't find any, just squeeze the juice of one lemon into the water.

SUBMITTED BY:
Susan Mihalo VanRiper

Brunch

Pittsburgh is a great town for brunch.

When we shot the promo for "'B' Is for Brunch" at the Grand Concourse over in Station Square, we couldn't believe the scores of families who arrived in wave after wave to browse the various stations for sweet and savory treats. Brunch is a great catch-all for everything from bagels with cream cheese and lox to omelettes, salads and breads of every type. We've included some classics like french toast and overnight dishes, but also some tasty surprises that you can spring on your guests during your next mid-morning feast.

Stuffed French Toast

INGREDIENTS

16 slices egg bread

16 oz. whipped cream cheese

8 oz. (1 c.) fruit preserves
(strawberry, blueberry,
raspberry)

6 eggs

1 c. cream

1 tsp. cinnamon

1 tsp. vanilla

1 Tbs. sugar

1/8 tsp. salt

4 c. corn flakes, crushed

2 Tbs. butter

Optional: confectioners' sugar

Plus: butter, maple syrup,
fruit sauce to taste

DIRECTIONS

Spread 8 of the bread slices with cream cheese and the other 8 with preserves. Put them together (with the fillings inside). Beat the eggs with the cream, cinnamon, vanilla, sugar and salt. Dip each sandwich into the batter to coat lightly. Then dip each into the crushed cornflakes to coat.

Melt the butter in a skillet or griddle over medium heat and fry the sandwiches until they are golden brown on both sides. Add more butter to the pan as needed. Remove the finished toast to a platter in a warm oven or a chafing dish.

Sprinkle with confectioners' sugar, if desired, and serve with more butter and warm maple syrup or fruit sauce.

SERVING
8

NOTES
You can make these up to an hour before serving and keep them warm in the oven. If you hold them much more than that, they begin to get tough.

SUBMITTED BY:
Chris Fennimore

Rolled Omelette

NOTES

This dish started out as part of a meatless meal for Lent, but it has become a favorite for Sunday brunches and even summer picnics.

SUBMITTED BY:
Chris Fennimore

INGREDIENTS

For the eggs
8 eggs
1 Tbs. olive oil
1/4 c. bread crumbs
1/4 c. grated romano cheese
2 Tbs. chopped fresh parsley
   or 2 tsp. dry
1/2 tsp. salt
1/4 tsp. oregano
1/4 tsp. black pepper
2 Tbs. milk
1 Tbs. margarine

For the salsa
2 medium tomatoes, seeded
   and diced
1/2 medium red onion, diced
1 clove garlic, minced
1 Tbs. olive oil
1 Tbs. balsamic vinegar
1 tsp. oregano
1/2 tsp. red pepper flakes
   (optional)
Salt and pepper

DIRECTIONS

For the eggs
   Beat the eggs with the oil. Stir in the bread crumbs, cheese, seasonings and milk.

   Heat a nonstick skillet over medium heat. Melt the margarine in the pan and then pour in the beaten egg mixture. Allow to cook for about 1 minute, until the bottom is golden brown.

   Carefully begin rolling the omelette from one side while pulling the rolled portion back to the edge of the pan, allowing the uncooked egg to refill the bottom of the pan. Keep rolling and pulling until you have formed the omelette into a cylinder.

   Roll it out onto a cutting board and cut into 1/2-inch slices on the diagonal. Return the slices to the pan and brown lightly on both sides. Serve with tomato salsa.

For the salsa
   Mix all the ingredients together except the salt and pepper. Allow to sit for at least a half hour. Add salt and black pepper to taste.

Windrift Farm Scrambled Eggs

INGREDIENTS

1 (7-oz.) can salad shrimp

1 (71/2-oz.) can crabmeat

6 Tbs. butter

2 Tbs. flour

3/4 c. milk

1 Tbs. fresh chives, chopped

12 eggs

31/2 Tbs. dry sherry

Pinch of tarragon

1 tsp. salt

DIRECTIONS

Drain shrimp and crab. Melt 2 tablespoons of butter in skillet and add flour. Stir until thick. Slowly add milk and simmer for 1 minute. Add chives and seafood. Set aside.

Whisk together eggs, sherry and seasonings. Melt the rest of the butter in skillet. Add eggs and stir until halfway cooked. Add seafood mixture and continue cooking until set.

Serve immediately.

SERVING

6

NOTES

As Alyson Sprague says, you'll never want to eat "plain" scrambled eggs again after you've tasted this simple but elegant version.

SUBMITTED BY:
Alyson Sprague

Best-Ever Irish Scones With Lemon Curd

SERVING
Makes about 2 dozen

NOTES
These scones can provide the core of your own tea party. Put out an assortment of preserves and maybe a tray of shortbread cookies. You'll feel like a character on "Masterpiece Theatre."

SUBMITTED BY:
Barbara Knezovich

INGREDIENTS

For the scones:

4 c. flour

1 c. sugar

4 tsp. baking powder

1/2 c. (1 stick) butter

1 c. golden raisins

2 eggs, beaten

11/2 c. buttermilk

For the lemon curd:

3 eggs

1/3 c. fresh lemon juice
  (3 lemons)

1 Tbs. finely shredded
  lemon zest

3/4 c. granulated sugar

6 Tbs. butter

DIRECTIONS

For the scones:

Preheat oven to 400°. Mix dry ingredients. Cut in butter. Add raisins. Place mixture in processor and slowly add eggs and enough buttermilk to make the dough roll around the blade. Roll dough into a circle about 1-inch thick. Cut with floured biscuit cutter.

Bake on an ungreased cookie sheet until slightly golden, about 15 minutes. Serve with lemon curd.

For the lemon curd:

In a nonreactive medium saucepan over low heat, whisk eggs, sugar, lemon juice and zest constantly, until the mixture is thick. Remove from heat and pour into a bowl. Cut the butter into small pieces and whisk into mixture until the butter is melted.

Cover and refrigerate. The lemon curd will keep for several days refrigerated.

Frittata

Ingredients

3 medium potatoes

3 Tbs. canola oil

1 onion, diced

6 eggs

1/2 c. grated romano cheese

2 Tbs. chopped parsley

1/2 tsp. oregano

Salt and pepper to taste

Garnish: tomato wedges,
 olive oil, basil

Directions

Peel the potatoes and cut them into 1/4-inch dice. Dry them with paper towels. Heat the oil in a 10- or 12-inch nonstick skillet. Saute the potatoes, turning frequently until they are golden-brown on all sides and tender. Add the onion, and continue frying until they are soft.

Beat the eggs in a large bowl. Add the cheese, parsley, oregano, salt and pepper. Pour the onions and potatoes into the egg mixture and stir until coated. Pour the mixture back into the pan and spread out the potatoes with a spatula. Cover and cook over moderate temperature until the bottom is golden-brown and the top is set. Carefully loosen the edges of the frittata and slide it out onto a large plate, cooked-side down. Invert the frying pan over the plate and flip over to cook the other side. Cook over moderate heat until the bottom is golden and slide out onto serving platter.

Serve with a garnish of fresh tomato wedges that have been tossed with olive oil, basil and a little salt and pepper.

Serving
4

Notes
There are thousands of possible variations on this Italian omelette. Try using some chopped fresh sage and grated asiago cheese. You can also use this recipe to clear the refrigerator of little bits of meat and vegetable leftovers.

Submitted by:
Chris Fennimore

Tomato and Bread Gratin

INGREDIENTS

11/4 lbs. cherry tomatoes

31/2 c. 1-inch cubes of
day-old bread

3-6 slivered garlic cloves

1/2 c. chopped parsley

1/2 tsp. pepper

2 Tbs. olive oil

1/2 tsp. salt

1/4 c. parmesan cheese

DIRECTIONS

Preheat oven to 375°.

Place tomatoes into a bowl and mix in remaining ingredients. Transfer to a 11/2 quart ovenproof gratin dish.

Bake for 40 minutes. Serve hot.

SERVING
4

NOTES
The olive oil is in here for taste, so make sure you use top quality.

SUBMITTED BY:
Jim Baran

Honey Mustard Dill Rye Bread (IN A BREAD MACHINE)

INGREDIENTS

1/2 c. water

1/4 c. chicken broth

2 1/2 Tbs. honey

1 2/3 Tbs. Dijon mustard

1 1/2 c. white flour

1/2 c. rye flour

2 tsp. dry milk

1/2 tsp. salt

1 tsp. dill

2 tsp. dry yeast

DIRECTIONS

Put ingredients in bread machine with wet ingredients on the bottom followed by dry ingredients and finally the yeast.

Let 'er spin.

NOTES

If you don't have a bread machine, double the ingredients. Then dissolve the yeast in the water, warmed to 110°, and mix with the other ingredients. Let it rise, then shape into a loaf. Let it rise again, and brush with an egg wash before baking. You'll have a beautiful, rustic-looking loaf.

SUBMITTED BY:
Chris Fennimore

Blueberry Chutney

Serving
Makes 8 half-pint jars

Notes
This unusual relish is particularly good with pork and ham. Mixed with mayonnaise or yogurt, it makes a piquant dressing for fruit salad or cold meat salads.

Submitted by:
Chris Fennimore

Ingredients

2 lbs. (2 pints) ripe blueberries, lightly crushed

1 1/2 c. red wine vinegar

1/4 lb. (1 medium) onion, peeled and finely chopped

1/2 c. golden raisins

1/2 c. packed, light-brown sugar

2 tsp. yellow mustard seed

1 Tbs. grated crystallized ginger

1/2 tsp. cinnamon

Pinch of salt

Pinch of ground nutmeg

1/2 tsp. dried crushed red pepper

Directions

Place all ingredients in a 4-quart saucepan (preferably not aluminum).

Bring to a boil over medium heat, stirring often.

Boil steadily, stirring occasionally until thick—about 45 minutes.

Spoon into hot, sterilized half-pint jars and seal.

Store in a cool spot when thoroughly cooled.

Baked Salmon With Creole Mustard Sauce

INGREDIENTS

For the sauce:

1 c. whipping cream

3/4 c. Creole mustard

4 tsp. Worchestershire sauce

1 Tbs. Dijon mustard

3/4 tsp. ground black pepper

1/4 tsp. ground white pepper

1/4 tsp. cayenne pepper

1/2 tsp. dried basil

1 c. sour cream

For the fish:

2 1/2 lb. center-cut salmon filets

1/4 c. melted unsalted butter

3 Tbs. brown sugar

3 Tbs. soy sauce

2 Tbs. white wine

2 Tbs. fresh lemon juice

DIRECTIONS

For the sauce:

Combine all ingredients except sour cream in a heavy saucepan. Simmer until thick (about 5 minutes), stirring frequently. Can be prepared a day ahead, covered, refrigerated, and reheated. Just before serving, add sour cream and whisk over low heat. When serving, pass separately.

For the fish:

Line a large baking pan with foil. Arrange fish, skin-side down, in single layer. Mix butter, sugar, soy sauce, lemon juice and wine in bowl. Pour over fish. Cover and refrigerate at least 1 hour, and up to 6 hours. Preheat oven to 400°. Uncover fish and bake just until cooked through, basting occasionally with pan drippings (about 18 minutes).

SERVING
6

NOTES
The Creole mustard is available in most supermarkets. You can substitute any coarse ground spicy mustard.

SUBMITTED BY:
Nancy Polinsky

Cheddar Cheese and Egg Brunch Casserole

SERVING
8

NOTES
You can add 1 pound of coarsely chopped ham or browned breakfast sausage with the cheese.

SUBMITTED BY:
Penny Lawrence

INGREDIENTS

16 slices white bread, crusts removed

8 oz. coarsely grated sharp cheddar cheese*

6 large eggs, beaten

1/2 tsp. salt, pepper to taste

3/4 tsp. dry mustard

1/4 c. minced onion

1/4 c. minced red bell pepper

1 1/2 tsp. Worcestershire sauce

Pinch of cayenne

3 c. whole milk

1 stick (1/2 c.) unsalted butter, melted

1 1/2 c. crushed potato chips

DIRECTIONS

Brush a 9x13-inch baking dish with a bit of butter. Line with 8 slices of bread. Sprinkle the bread with the cheese. Place another layer of bread over the cheese. In a bowl, combine the beaten eggs, salt, pepper, mustard, onion, red pepper, Worcestershire sauce and cayenne. After combining these well, add the milk. Spoon this mixture over the bread in the prepared pan. Cover with plastic wrap and refrigerate overnight.

Just before baking, spoon the melted butter over the top of the casserole and top with the potato chips. Bake in a preheated 350° oven, uncovered, for 60 minutes.

Strawberry Tea Bread

INGREDIENTS

3 c. all-purpose flour

1 1/2 Tbs. ground cinnamon

1 tsp. baking soda

1 tsp. salt

2 c. sugar

4 eggs, beaten

1 1/4 c. vegetable oil

2 c. fresh (or frozen)
strawberries, slightly mashed

1 1/2 c. chopped pecans

DIRECTIONS

Grease two 8x5x3-inch loaf pans. Preheat oven to 350°.

Combine dry ingredients. Add eggs, oil, strawberries and pecans. Blend until all is moistened.

Divide batter between pans and bake for 60-70 minutes, until a toothpick inserted comes out dry.

SERVING
Makes 2 loaves

NOTES
This is another great addition to your afternoon tea celebration. If you use fresh strawberries, mash them and let them macerate with a little of the sugar from the recipe for about an hour.
This will bring out the juices and natural flavors of the berries.

SUBMITTED BY:
Antoinette Jucha

Summer Fun

Sausage rolls, ❖ page 39;
Hot sausage soup, ❖ page 68

The lazy, hazy days of summer also mean cookouts and picnics and days at the beach. We've included some barbecue specialties, a handful of salads and some very cool soups that will make the living easy. The best thing about summer is the abundance of fresh fruits and vegetables, and these recipes take every advantage of nature's summer abundance. Tomatoes will never be juicier or raspberries sweeter. Other than the slow barbecue roasting, most of these recipes can be made ahead, and that provides one of the greatest pleasures of the season: free time.

Sausage Rolls

INGREDIENTS

1 1/2 lb. ground pork

1 Tbs. fennel seed

1 tsp. salt

1/4 tsp. pepper

1 Tbs. red pepper flakes
  (optional)

1 c. grated provolone

1 c. grated mozzarella

1/2 c. grated romano

1 (1-lb.) batch of pizza dough or
  frozen bread dough

Olive oil

Paprika (optional)

DIRECTIONS

Saute the ground pork until well-browned. Drain excess fat. Allow to cool slightly, then add the fennel seeds, spices and cheeses.

Cut the dough into 16 bun-size pieces. Flatten each piece into a roughly round shape and top with 2 tablespoons of the meat/cheese mixture. Fold the bottom edge toward the middle, tuck in the two sides and continue to roll up until you have enclosed the mixture. Pinch the seam together and place seam-side down on a greased or parchment-covered baking sheet. Allow to rise for about a half-hour.

Brush gently with olive oil and mark with a sprinkling of paprika if you have included the hot pepper flakes. Bake at 350° for 20 minutes or until golden-brown.

SERVING
Makes 16

NOTES
My brothers are fond of splitting these as if they were buns, and making a sandwich with roasted red peppers and a slice of provolone. I've been known to put a dab of hot mustard on them as if they were soft pretzels.

SUBMITTED BY:
Chris Fennimore

Oven-Roasted Barbecue Brisket

SERVING
8

NOTES
This marinating paste is somewhere between a dry rub and a sauce. It serves just as well for chicken and pork, and you can add a little extra heat with the addition of some cayenne pepper.

SUBMITTED BY:
Roy Haley

INGREDIENTS

For the brisket:

4-6 lbs. beef brisket

Marinating paste (see below)

2-3 c. barbecue sauce

1 large onion sliced into
    thick rings and separated

For the marinating paste:

1 Tbs. salt

1 Tbs. onion salt

1 Tbs. garlic salt

1 Tbs. black pepper

2 Tbs. celery seed or
    celery salt

2 Tbs. Worcestershire sauce

1 Tbs. liquid smoke

DIRECTIONS

Trim brisket. Mix all marinade ingredients and cover all sides of brisket with paste. Place in foil-lined pan, fat-side up, cover tightly and refrigerate overnight, or a minimum of 4 hours.

Preheat oven to 300°. Cook brisket 1 hour per pound. With 1 hour left to cook, remove from oven and pour off juices. Cover with barbecue sauce and the onion rings, then re-cover with foil and return to oven for remaining hour. Remove from oven and let stand for 10 minutes.

Slice brisket across the grain in 1/4-inch slices. Top brisket with more barbecue sauce, or serve on the side.

Grilled Turkey Breast (WITH ORANGE AND ROSEMARY)

INGREDIENTS

2 large shallots, finely chopped

1/2 c. orange juice

3 Tbs. olive oil

3 Tbs. chopped fresh rosemary
or 2 tsp. dried, crumbled

2 Tbs. balsamic vinegar

4 tsp. grated orange peel

1 Tbs. honey

1 tsp. salt

1/8 tsp. dried crushed red pepper

2 lbs. skinless, boneless turkey
breast half

DIRECTIONS

Place all ingredients except turkey in a large plastic bag. Seal bag and shake gently to mix. Place turkey between 2 sheets of plastic wrap and flatten with a meat pounder until 1-inch thick all over. Remove plastic wrap, place turkey in bag with marinade and seal. Refrigerate 6-12 hours. Remove turkey from bag.

Bring marinade to a boil and brush over turkey during grilling. Grill meat over medium heat until center registers 155°, about 12 minutes per side. Transfer turkey to a warm platter, cover with foil, and let stand 20 minutes before serving.

SERVING
4

NOTES
Remember to bring the marinade to a boil for a few minutes before using it as a basting sauce. Then just add cole slaw and potato salad for a perfect summer menu.

SUBMITTED BY:
Jim Baran

Potato-Crusted Halibut (WITH CITRUS SAUCE)

SERVING
4

NOTES
Ever since chef
Greg Alauzen showed us
how to make this during
the "Quick and Easy"
marathon, it's been one of
my favorites. Try using
other fish, such as orange
roughy or tilapia.

SUBMITTED BY:
Chef Greg Alauzen

INGREDIENTS

2 c. fresh orange juice

Juice of 1 lime

Juice of 1 lemon

4 large Idaho potatoes,
peeled and stored in water

4 (6- to 7-oz.) steaks of
fresh halibut

Kosher salt to taste

Freshly ground black pepper
to taste

Wondra flour to taste

Blended oil: 75% canola,
25% extra virgin olive oil

1 lb. fresh spinach, trimmed
and washed

4-6 Tbs. butter

About 1 Tbs. fresh chives
sliced thin (save 8 chive sticks
for garnish.)

DIRECTIONS

In a small saucepan, combine orange, lime and lemon
juices. Bring to boil and reduce heat to gentle boil.
Reduce amount by half.

Grate potatoes onto a kitchen towel. Rinse quickly in cold
water and wring to dry. Arrange fish on cookie sheet and
lightly season with salt and pepper. Cover with potatoes and
then season potatoes lightly with salt, pepper and small
amount of the Wondra. Add enough oil to a heated saute
pan to form a thin layer. As oil just starts to smoke, scoop
fish with spatula and put into pan potato-side down.
Cook until golden-brown and flip onto cookie sheet fish-side
down. Place in 400° oven for about 8 minutes.
Fish should be firm.

Heat large saute pan with small amount of oil, and add
spinach. Lightly season with salt and pepper. Finish
juice/sauce by whisking in butter. Season with thinly sliced
chives. Place spinach in center of plate, fish on top and
sauce around the plate. Garnish with extra chives and serve.

Horseradish Potato Salad

INGREDIENTS

8 medium new potatoes

4 Tbs. lemon juice

4 Tbs. vegetable oil

Salt to taste

1/2 tsp. freshly ground
   black pepper

2 celery ribs, chopped

3 Tbs. finely chopped onion

1- 1 1/4 c. mayonnaise

3 Tbs. cider vinegar

2 Tbs. minced dill

2 Tbs. horseradish, either
   freshly grated or bottled

2 hard-boiled eggs, thinly sliced

DIRECTIONS

Boil potatoes just until tender when pierced with a fork. Drain, peel and dice or slice. Gently toss with lemon juice, oil and salt to taste. Cool potato mixture.

Mix together the pepper, celery, onion, mayo, vinegar, dill and horseradish. Add dressing mixture, a little at a time, to the cooled potato mixture. Gently toss, adding more dressing, until all potatoes are well-covered.

Garnish with sliced eggs. Serve immediately, or keep well-chilled until ready to serve.

SERVING
4

NOTES
Mashed potatoes with a dollop of horseradish are all the rage, so it's not surprising to see a salad recipe based on the same idea.

SUBMITTED BY:
Jim Baran

Carrot Salad

SERVING
4

NOTES

Mom never made this salad until she, Dad and Gram moved down to Florida in 1977. Since it has tropical ingredients like coconut and pineapple, I guess she thought it was appropriate.

SUBMITTED BY:
Chris Fennimore

INGREDIENTS

2 lbs. carrots, grated

1 c. golden raisins

4 Tbs. orange juice concentrate

4 Tbs. mayonnaise

2 (8-oz.) cans crushed pineapple, drained

1/2 c. shredded coconut

1/2 c. roasted sunflower seeds

DIRECTIONS

You just need to toss all the ingredients together and let them marinate for a little while to mix all the flavors.

Sprinkle on the sunflower seeds at the last minute so they retain their crunchiness.

Greek Orzo Salad With Shrimp

INGREDIENTS

For the dressing:
1/4 c. fresh dill
1/4 c. + 1 Tbs. fresh mint
1 clove garlic
1 oz. red onion
3 Tbs. olive oil
1 1/2 Tbs. white wine vinegar
1/2 tsp. salt
Pepper to taste

For the salad:
1 lb. large shrimp, peeled
    and cooked
1/2 c. orzo
1 tsp. vegetable oil
3 oz. feta
1 large tomato, seeded and diced
12 Calamata olives, pitted and
    chopped
2 green onions, sliced
Green, red and yellow bell
    pepper strips
1 zucchini, sliced
Red leaf lettuce
Fresh dill sprigs
Toasted pine nuts

DIRECTIONS

For the dressing:

Place dill and mint in a food processor. With the machine running, add the garlic and onion. Process until minced, scraping down sides of bowl. Add oil, lemon juice, vinegar and salt. Season with pepper. Process until blended, about 5 seconds. Transfer dressing to a large bowl.

For the salad:

Cook orzo. Rinse and drain, then toss with oil. When cool, add to dressing along with shrimp, cheese, tomato, olives, onions, peppers and zucchini. Toss gently to combine. Adjust seasoning. Cover and refrigerate. Salad can be prepared 3 hours in advance.

Line serving plates with lettuce. Mound salad atop lettuce. Garnish with dill and pine nuts.

SERVING
4

NOTES
Orzo is a tiny, rice-shaped pasta. You should be able to find it near the other macaroni in the supermarket. In a pinch, you can just use a cup of cooked rice.

SUBMITTED BY:
Jim Baran

Celery and Olive Salad

INGREDIENTS

1 head of celery

1/4 c. olive oil

1/4 c. white wine vinegar

Black pepper to taste

1 c. cracked olives

DIRECTIONS

Clean the celery stalks and cut into 1/4-inch slices. Put into a large bowl with the oil, vinegar and black pepper.

Remove the pits from the olives by hitting them with the bottom of a heavy coffee mug on a chopping board. Cut the olive meat into pieces about the size of the celery. Add the olives to the celery mixture and marinate for at least an hour or overnight.

Serve as a side dish for lunch or as part of an antipasto.

SERVING
6

NOTES
We used to add oregano, basil, fennel seeds and hot pepper flakes to this salad, but the cracked olives I get in the Strip District are already swimming in those spices.

SUBMITTED BY:
Chris Fennimore

Cold Blueberry Soup

INGREDIENTS

6 c. blueberries

5 c. water

1 c. sugar

2 medium lemons, thinly sliced

1 3-inch cinnamon stick

1/2 tsp. freshly grated nutmeg

1/4 tsp. allspice

41/2 c. sour cream

1 c. dry red wine

DIRECTIONS

Combine blueberries, water, sugar, lemons and spices in a large saucepan and bring to boil over high heat. Reduce heat to medium-low and simmer uncovered 15 minutes.

Strain mixture into large bowl, discarding cinnamon stick and lemon slices. Cover and chill thoroughly.

Just before serving, whisk in sour cream and wine.

SERVING
10-12

NOTES
The soup can be prepared the day before; just stir in the sour cream and wine before serving.
It's a cool treat for a hot summer day.

SUBMITTED BY:
Penny Lawrence

Gazpacho

INGREDIENTS

1/2 c. diced celery

1/2 c. diced green peppers

1/2 c. diced onion

1/2 c. diced cucumber

1/2 c. diced tomatoes

1 (10.5-oz.) can tomato soup

1 can water

1 Tbs. Italian dressing

1 tsp. black pepper

1 dash Worcestershire sauce

1 1/2 c. V-8 juice
   (or a 11.5-oz. can)

1 Tbs. wine vinegar

Garlic powder to taste

4 dashes Tabasco sauce

DIRECTIONS

Combine all ingredients and refrigerate.

SERVING
4

NOTES
Here's a tasty way to get your full daily requirement of vegetables in one tangy, refreshing dish.

SUBMITTED BY:
Nancy Polinsky

Freezer Berry Jam

INGREDIENTS

6 c. whole berries
  (about 4 c. crushed)
3¹/4 c. sugar
1 (1.75-oz.) package
  Sure-Jell pectin

DIRECTIONS

Wash and hull the berries. Crush them 1 cup at a time (not too much if you like big pieces of fruit in your jam). Mix ¹/4 cup of the sugar with the powdered pectin. Slowly add this to the crushed berries while stirring vigorously. I don't know if this helps, but it makes you feel as if you're doing something during this incredibly simple recipe. Let this stand for 30 minutes, stirring once or twice during that time. Now slowly add the 3 cups of sugar and stir until completely dissolved. If possible, get a child to do this: It builds character and forearm muscles.

Wash six 8-oz. canning jars and their lids, and rinse with really hot water. Fill each jar to within ¹/2 inch of the top. Wipe the tops and threads clean, and put on the lids and screw top. Allow to stand at room temperature for 24 hours, and then store in the freezer.

When you open them, you won't believe the fresh fruit flavor that just bursts from the jars. Great on toast, scones, waffles, ice cream, etc.

SERVING
Makes 6 half-pint jars

NOTES
This is a great recipe to have on hand after you've loaded the trunk full of berries at one of those "pick your own" local farms.

SUBMITTED BY:
Chris Fennimore

Vegetables and Meatless

Couscous, apricot and
pistachio salad, ❖ page 53

Food

experts, dietitians and medical experts are encouraging everyone to eat more vegetables. If you want to get in five or more servings per day, it's nice to have a repertoire of quick, easy and delicious vegetable recipes. There's nothing wrong with steamed broccoli, but you wouldn't want to eat it every night for a week. Over the course of our "QED Cooks" programs, we've gathered a tremendous number of inventive ways to prepare vegetables as side dishes, casseroles and main courses. Here are about a dozen good ideas that will spice up your menus.

Couscous, Apricot and Pistachio Salad

INGREDIENTS

2 c. couscous

2 tsp. cinnamon

1/2 tsp. allspice

1 c. dried apricots, sliced thin

3 c. water or chicken stock

1/4 c. olive oil

1 tsp. salt

1 bunch scallions

4 Tbs. chopped fresh basil

1/2 c. shelled and toasted
   pistachio nuts

DIRECTIONS

In a large bowl, mix the couscous with the cinnamon, allspice and apricots.

Combine the water, oil and salt in a saucepan; bring to a boil and pour over the couscous. Stir to blend, then cover for 5 minutes.

Uncover and fluff with a fork. Allow to cool. (You can refrigerate this for a day or so until you want to serve the salad, but let it come to room temperature before adding the other ingredients and serving.)

Chop the scallions finely and the basil roughly. Toss into the couscous and add the pistachios at the last minute.

SERVING
8

NOTES
If you buy the nuts already shelled, it's best to toast them for just a few minutes to bring out their flavor and crunchy texture.

SUBMITTED BY:
Chris Fennimore

Couscous with Pesto Flavors

INGREDIENTS

3 c. chicken stock

1 tsp. salt

1/4 c. olive oil

1 clove garlic, minced

2 c. couscous

1 c. grated parmigiana or romano cheese

1/2 c. fresh basil, minced

1 c. tomatoes, seeded and diced

1/2 c. toasted pignoli nuts

Juice of 1 lemon

Garnish: fresh basil

DIRECTIONS

Combine the chicken stock, salt, olive oil and garlic in a saucepan, and bring to a boil. Remove from heat and add the couscous. Stir to blend; cover. After 5 minutes, fluff with a fork.

At this point, you can add the rest of the ingredients for a warm side dish, or cool the couscous for a salad.

When cool, add the cheese, basil, tomatoes and nuts. Fluff with a fork.

Just before serving, sprinkle with the lemon juice and a few extra sprigs of basil.

SERVING
8

NOTES
Grill some chicken breasts that you've brushed with olive oil and dusted with salt and basil. Then slice them into strips and fan them out over the couscous for a fabulous buffet platter.

SUBMITTED BY:
Chris Fennimore

Red Vegetarian Chili

INGREDIENTS

2 1/2 to 3 Tbs. extra-virgin olive oil

3/4 medium onion, finely chopped

1/2 tsp. turmeric

3/4 c. orange or red pepper, diced

2 (15.5-oz.) cans kidney beans, drained

3 plum tomatoes, chopped

1 (6-oz.) can tomato paste (I prefer
    Contadina brand)

1 (14.5-oz.) can Contadina diced
    tomatoes, roasted garlic flavor

Pinch of salt

1 c. water

2 Tbs. (or more to taste) Taco Bell or
    McCormick Mild Taco Seasoning

Pinch of ground black pepper

2 Tbs. Heinz red tomato ketchup

2 Tbs. Ovaltine, chocolate malt flavor

1 Tbs. lemon juice

Sprinkling of dried basil, dill, sage
    and thyme

Fresh cilantro

DIRECTIONS

Heat olive oil in a large shallow pan on medium heat. Add chopped onion, and saute until translucent. Add the turmeric, stir, then add chopped pepper. Turn heat to low. Add drained kidney beans. Turn heat to medium, and add the tomatoes, tomato paste, diced tomatoes and salt. Mix well to ensure even cooking. After a minute, add the water and mix well. Then add taco seasoning, pepper, ketchup, and Ovaltine. Mix, then add lemon juice, dried seasonings, and a small portion of the chopped cilantro.

Keep the pan on heat for a few minutes, then taste to determine whether the kidney beans have absorbed the flavors. Keep the pan on the stove until this is the case.

Just before removing the chili from the stove, add more chopped fresh cilantro and stir well. Serve warm.

Garnish:

Chopped onions, shredded sharp cheddar, chopped cilantro and chopped tomatoes

SERVING
4

NOTES
I remember sending in Ovaltine labels for a Captain Midnight decoder ring. Who knew the stuff would make a delicious addition to chili? Maybe it will make a comeback.

SUBMITTED BY:
Rami Rao

Tofu Chili

INGREDIENTS

2 lbs. firm tofu

1/4 c. soy sauce

1 1/2 Tbs. tomato paste

2 Tbs. peanut butter

1/2 Tbs. onion powder

1/4 Tbs. garlic powder

1/2 c. water

1/4 c. plus 4 Tbs. oil

1 large green pepper, diced

2 large onions, diced

3 cloves garlic, minced

5 c. canned pinto beans,
   reserve liquid

1 Tbs. salt

3 Tbs. chili powder

1 1/2 Tbs. cumin

DIRECTIONS

Freeze, thaw, then squeeze and tear the tofu into bite-sized pieces. Mix the soy sauce, tomato paste, peanut butter, onion and garlic powders, water and 2 tablespoons of the oil. Stir in the tofu pieces until well-coated, then fry in 1/4 cup of oil until all liquid is absorbed and tofu is well-browned.

In another pan, saute the peppers, onions and garlic in 2 tablespoons of oil until the onions are transparent. Combine the vegetables, browned tofu and drained beans in a large pot. Add enough of the reserved liquid to cover. Season with salt, chili powder and cumin. Bring to a simmer and serve hot with crusty bread.

SERVING
6

NOTES
Freezing and then thawing the tofu gives it a totally different consistency. It's almost spongelike in the way it soaks up the flavors and liquids in which it is cooked.

SUBMITTED BY:
Jay Bernard

Stuffed Grape Leaves (Warak Inrb Mishay)

INGREDIENTS

1/2 lb. coarsely ground lamb

1/2 lb. ground round steak

1/2 c. long grain rice

2 tsp. clarified butter

Salt and pepper to taste

25-35 grape leaves

1 potato, sliced

1 lemon slice

2 cloves garlic

Salt to taste

Juice of 1 lemon

DIRECTIONS

Combine meats with rice, butter, salt, pepper and set aside.

If using fresh grape leaves, rinse well and place in pan of hot water. Turn off heat and allow leaves to soften for 10 minutes. Squeeze out excess moisture.

Use medium-sized tender leaves. If small, use two, overlapping a little. Place a rounded teaspoon of filling at the stem end of leaf. Spread out to form a line. Tuck in the sides and roll away from you, forming a thin tube. Repeat with each leaf until the filling is used up.

Put a few slices of raw potato in the bottom of a saucepan along with a slice of lemon and the garlic cloves. Arrange the rolled leaves in the pot, alternating the direction of each row. Sprinkle with salt and lemon juice and weigh down with plate and saucer of water. Add enough water to cover the plate. Bring to a boil, lower heat and simmer for 30-40 minutes.

SERVING

6

NOTES

You can serve these cool or at room temperature as part of a maza platter with hummus and baba ghanoush, or warm as a main course.

SUBMITTED BY:
Marian Albert

Vegetable Stew

INGREDIENTS

1 c. dried white beans

3 c. water

3 onions, chopped

1 clove garlic, minced

1/2 c. chopped celery

4 medium tomatoes, chopped

1 small green pepper, seeded
  and chopped

1/2 tsp. dried basil, or
  fresh basil

2 medium zucchini, chopped

Salt and pepper to taste

Garnish: parsley

DIRECTIONS

Rinse beans and soak overnight in 3 cups of water.

Cook beans in the soaking water for 1 hour. Drain beans, then mix with the onions, garlic, celery, tomatoes, pepper and basil.

Transfer to casserole. Cover and bake at 350° for 1¹/2 hours.

Add zucchini and cook uncovered for 20 minutes.

Add salt and pepper. Garnish with parsley, if desired.

SERVING
4

NOTES
You could also soak the beans overnight, but don't go much over 12 hours, or the beans will get mushy.

SUBMITTED BY:
Catherine Monte Carlo

Eggplant Sauce for Pasta

INGREDIENTS

1 garlic clove, minced

2 Tbs. fresh chopped basil

1 medium eggplant, sliced but
   left unpeeled

1/2 c. sliced fresh mushrooms

4 c. whole canned tomatoes

Salt and pepper to taste

DIRECTIONS

Put on the water for pasta, then heat a nonstick skillet and spray with a nonstick cooking spray.

Add chopped garlic and basil.

Add eggplant slices and cook until they begin to soften.

Add mushrooms and begin to saute, then break tomatoes into large pieces and add to the mixture. Simmer 10 minutes with lid on, 10 without. Salt and pepper to taste.

Serve hot over pasta.

SERVING

4

NOTES

This is one of those recipes that is ready in the time that it takes to boil macaroni. You can easily make it from scratch after you get home from work.

SUBMITTED BY:

Barbara Knezovich

Pittsburgh Potatoes

INGREDIENTS

1 (2-lb.) bag Ore-Ida Southern
    Style Hash Browns potatoes
1 (8-oz.) package shredded
    sharp cheese
1 (10.5-oz.) can cream of
    chicken soup
1/2 c. (1 stick) butter, melted
About 1 c. (more to taste)
    crushed potato chips
    for topping

DIRECTIONS

Preheat oven to 350°. In large bowl, mix together frozen potatoes, cheese, soup and melted butter.

Spray 9x11 baking dish with cooking spray.

Spread potato mixture evenly in pan.

Sprinkle with crushed potato chips.

Bake uncovered for 1 hour.

SERVING
8

NOTES
People have also sent in countless variations substituting cream of mushroom soup, crushed cornflakes, etc. They all disappear just as quickly.

SUBMITTED BY:
Denise Robbins

Finocchi al Pomodoro e Uvetta (FENNEL WITH TOMATOES & RAISINS)

INGREDIENTS

2 Tbs. olive oil

6 fennel bulbs

1 small yellow onion

6 ripe plum tomatoes

1/2 c. raisins

1 tsp. cumin seeds

DIRECTIONS

Heat the olive oil in a large saute pan. Trim the tops of the fennel bulbs and cut each into 4 pieces.

Chop the onion and add it to the saute pan.

After a minute or two, add the fennel. Stir until the onion and fennel have wilted and almost begun to brown.

Chop the tomatoes; add to the pan with the raisins and cumin seeds.

Lower the heat and cover.

Simmer for 30-40 minutes until the fennel is tender.

SERVING
6

NOTES
Can be served warm or at room temperature. (Great accompaniment for fish dishes.)

SUBMITTED BY:
Chris Fennimore

Broccoli-Cauliflower Casserole

Serving
6-8

Notes
Nancy took some good-natured ribbing for bringing in this recipe using Cheez Whiz, but there wasn't a crumb left after she served it.

Submitted by:
Nancy Polinsky

Ingredients

1/2 c. (1 stick) margarine

1 stack (package) Ritz crackers

1 (10-oz.) package frozen broccoli

1 (10-oz.) package frozen cauliflower

1 (8-oz.) jar Cheez Whiz

Directions

Preheat oven to 350°.

Melt margarine, crush crackers into crumbs and mix with margarine.

Place vegetables into casserole.

Spread with Cheez Whiz.

Spread crumbs over top.

Bake 20-30 minutes or until bubbly and golden.

Broccoli-Corn Bake

INGREDIENTS

1 (16-oz.) can creamed corn

1 (10-oz.) package chopped frozen broccoli, cooked and drained

1 beaten egg

1 Tbs. instant minced onion OR 1/4 c. finely chopped onion

1/2 tsp. salt

Dash pepper

12 coarsely crumbled Ritz crackers (about 1/2 c.)

2 Tbs. butter or margarine, melted

6 more coarsely crumbled Ritz crackers (about 1/4 c.)

1 Tbs. butter or margarine, melted

DIRECTIONS

Preheat oven to 350°.

Combine vegetables, egg, seasonings, the 1/2 cup of crackers and 2 tablespoons of butter.

Turn into 1-quart casserole dish.

Mix remaining crackers and butter; sprinkle over casserole.

Bake uncovered for 35-40 minutes.

SERVING

6

NOTES

This is similar to Nancy's casserole with its Ritz crackers topping, but the creamed corn and egg give this a different texture.

SUBMITTED BY:
Chris Fennimore

Comfort Foods

Macaroni and cheese, ❖ page 67

One

of these days we're going to have to devote an entire marathon to the subject of comfort foods. Everyone has his or her own idea of what that means. To some, it is mashed potatoes or macaroni and cheese. To others, comfort comes in the form of bubbling pots of soups and stews. What's common to almost everyone is that these foods are rooted in childhood memories. The warmth and texture of the dishes may give us physical pleasure, but the connections with happy times and the ones we love are what provide the true feelings of comfort that continue to make us crave these meals when we need a little solace

Macaroni and Cheese

INGREDIENTS

2¹/2 c. cooked elbow macaroni

3 c. grated sharp cheddar
   cheese

Salt and pepper to taste

Optional: paprika

1/2 stick butter or margarine

6 eggs

1 c. milk

1 (12.-oz.) can evaporated milk

DIRECTIONS

Preheat oven to 325°.

Cover the bottom of the casserole dish with 1 layer of macaroni. Top with a layer of the cheese. Sprinkle with salt and pepper and paprika if desired. Repeat layers until dish is full, ending with cheese on top.

Dot the top with pats of butter or margarine.

Mix eggs with milk and canned milk and season with salt and pepper. Pour over the casserole.

Bake until top is golden and the mixture is firm.

SERVING
6

NOTES
Pauline Lowery is one of the great Church Ladies of Pittsburgh. Her food has brought strength and comfort and fellowship to thousands.

SUBMITTED BY:
Pauline Lowery

Hot Sausage Soup

SERVING
6

NOTES
Using mustard greens gives this dish an especially zesty flavor. This is deep-winter food that will raise a sweat on any brow.

SUBMITTED BY:
Chris Fennimore

INGREDIENTS

1 1/2 lb. hot Italian sausage

1/2 c. water

1 large onion

1 green pepper

1 red pepper

1 (28-oz.) can crushed
    tomatoes

1 (28-oz.) can water

Salt and pepper

Bay leaf

4 cloves garlic

1 bunch greens
    (escarole, mustard, kale, etc.)

2 (15-oz.) cans cannellini
    beans

Optional: grated
    romano cheese

DIRECTIONS

Over medium-high heat, saute the sausage in the water in a large sauce pot until the water evaporates and the sausage is browned on all sides. While it's frying, pierce the sausage in several places with a fork to release some of the fat. Remove the sausage and cut into 1/2-inch rounds. Chop the onion and peppers into 1/2-inch chunks, and fry in the same pan until they are tender. Put the sausage rounds back into the pot and use a food mill to strain the crushed tomatoes into the pot. Add 1 can of water, salt, pepper, bay leaf and garlic cloves; bring to a boil, then lower to a simmer. Cook uncovered for about 1 1/2 hours.

Wash and chop the greens into bite-size pieces. Drain and rinse 1 can of the beans, and add to the soup. Puree the other can of beans; add to the soup along with the greens. Simmer for another 15 minutes until the greens are tender.

Serve with hunks of crusty bread. It's also nice to sprinkle each serving with a generous helping of grated romano cheese.

Pork and Cabbage Braise

INGREDIENTS

1 lb. lean, boneless pork

1 Tbs. olive oil

1 Tbs. butter

1/2 head medium cabbage,
   shredded

1 medium onion, diced

2 tsp. caraway seeds

Salt and pepper to taste

1/2 c. white wine

1 c. low-fat chicken stock

1 red pepper, cut into strips

1 green pepper, cut into strips

DIRECTIONS

Cut the meat into julienne strips. Heat the tablespoon of olive oil in a large skillet, and saute the pork quickly until browned. Remove the meat to a bowl and add the butter to the pan.

Reduce the heat to medium and saute the cabbage until wilted. Add the onion and continue cooking until the onion is tender. Add the caraway seeds, salt, ground pepper and wine. Raise the heat to high and cook until almost all the wine is evaporated. Pour in the chicken stock, bring back to a boil and reduce to a simmer.

Add the meat and pepper strips, cover and simmer just until the peppers are crisp tender.

Stir well and serve with noodles or spaetzle.

SERVING
6

NOTES

I have always added a little brown sugar and caraway seeds to my sauerkraut, so it only seemed natural to include it in this simple but satisfying cabbage dish.

SUBMITTED BY:
Chris Fennimore

Lone Rhino Chili

SERVING
At least 10

NOTES
Joe would probably encourage you NOT to follow this recipe, since he favors an improvisational approach to chili preparation. But it's a darn good starting point.

SUBMITTED BY:
Joe Fennimore

INGREDIENTS

1 1/2 lbs. assorted dry beans
  (pinto, pink, kidney, black, etc.)
3 medium onions, coarsely chopped
1 Tbs. olive oil
2 Tbs. chopped garlic
3 1/2 lbs. London broil, finely cubed
1 tsp. fennel seed
1 tsp. oregano
1 tsp. freshly ground black pepper
2 tsp. crushed red pepper
6 Tbs. chili powder
4 oz. Jack Daniels whiskey
1 c. dark beer, porter or stout
4 oz. cayenne pepper sauce
  (Franks, Texas Pete, Crystal, etc.)
1 c. black coffee
2 jalapeno peppers, finely chopped
1 poblano pepper, medium chop
2 Tbs. cumin
1 Tbs. dry pasilla pod
  (ancho chile), finely chopped
2 green bell peppers, big chunks
5 bottles dark beer, more as needed

DIRECTIONS

You'll need two pots to make the chili, a 16-20 quart and an 8-12 quart, both with lids. Rinse the beans and place in the smaller pot with about 4 quarts water. Bring to a boil, then reduce heat and simmer for 20 minutes. Drain and add new water to cover. Return to the boil and simmer for 1 hour.

While beans are simmering, saute the onions in the olive oil in the large pot until golden-brown. Add the garlic, then the meat, along with the fennel seed, oregano, black pepper, red pepper and 2 tablespoons of the chili powder. Cook at medium until the meat is browned. Pour in the Jack Daniels and 1 cup of dark beer. Reduce heat.

Add the beans to the meat and about one pint of the bean juice. Reserve the rest of the bean liquid. Add all the remaining ingredients except the green peppers and 5 bottles of dark beer. The peppers you add about 1 hour before serving, and the beer you drink while the chili simmers over the next 4 hours. Add water or bean juice to keep mixture "soupy" during the early stages of cooking.

Allow the chili to reduce and thicken toward the end of the cooking time. Serve with a buttered kaiser roll and more of that dark beer.

Chuck's Many-Peppered Chili

INGREDIENTS

6 Tbs. chili powder (or several
   reconstituted arbole chili peppers)
2 Tbs. chipotle powder or 3
   reconstituted dried peppers
2 Tbs. pasilla-negro powder or 2
   reconstituted dried peppers
3 Tbs. cumin
1 Tbs. tumeric
2 tsp. coriander
1 tsp. salt
1 tsp. black pepper
1 large yellow onion
1 green pepper
1 red pepper
2 anaheim peppers (seeded)
2 jalapeno peppers (seeded)
Optional: 1 habanero if you like
   high heat
4 (15-oz.) cans dark red kidney beans
1 lb. beef steak
1 lb. ground beef
1 lb. pork cutlets
1 lb. ground pork (andouille
   orchorizo sausage can be
   substituted)
4-6 cloves garlic (crushed)
2 (10.5-oz.) cans beef consomme
2 (14.5-oz.) cans diced tomatoes

DIRECTIONS

Gently toast peppers in a cast-iron skillet over medium heat until you can smell the chili aroma rising from the pan. Then open them up and remove the seeds and grind them to a powder. Of course, you can simply buy the powdered versions.

Measure and combine the spices. Chop up the onion and peppers (wear gloves while tackling the jalapeno and habanero) into a large dice and set aside. Open and drain the 4 cans of beans. Cut the beef and pork into bite-sized chunks. Put them and the ground beef into a large pot over medium high heat. Add the spices and brown the meat. Stir often, but try not to break the ground meats into tiny specks. Do not overcook the meat, but just until all the red is gone. Remove the meat from the pot and drain off the fat, leaving about 2 tablespoons in the pan. Add the diced onion and peppers, stirring and scraping to deglaze the pan. Cook for about 10 minutes, until the onion is translucent and the peppers are tender. Add the crushed garlic, stir and cook for another minute. Add the beef consomme, beans, tomatoes and the meat. Simmer for a few hours, stirring occasionally. Taste and adjust the seasonings as desired.

Serve over rice, polenta cakes, hominy or tortilla chips and garnish with any combination of shredded cheddar or monterey jack, sour cream, green onions, minced chives and black olives.

Garnish: shredded cheese, sour cream, green onions, chives, olives

SERVING
At least 10

NOTES
Unlike his elder brothers, Chuck is a kitchen scientist, honing recipes to a fine edge of flavor through repeated testing and adjustment. Every ingredient has its own special place in the final gustatory experience.

SUBMITTED BY:
Chuck Fennimore

Bean Casserole

NOTES

If you take these beans to a covered-dish event, remember to take extra copies of the recipe. Everyone will want to make it.

SUBMITTED BY:
Horace Miles

INGREDIENTS

2 lbs. ground beef

1 small onion, chopped

2 (27-oz.) cans baked beans

1 (15-oz). can butter beans, drained

1 (15-oz.) can kidney beans, drained

1/2 c. sugar

1/2 c. brown sugar

4 Tbs. Worcestershire sauce

2 Tbs. dry mustard

2/3 c. ketchup

DIRECTIONS

Brown ground beef with onion and drain.

Mix all ingredients in a large casserole.

Bake at 300° for 1 1/2 hours.

Buffalo chicken chili, ❖ page 75;
Honey mustard dill rye bread, ❖ page 31

A-Ole ❖ page 76

Buffalo Chicken Chili

INGREDIENTS

3 Tbs. cayenne pepper sauce
  (Red Devil, Franks,
  Texas Pete, etc.)

3 boneless chicken breasts

1/4 c. flour

4 Tbs. butter

3 stalks celery, diced

1/2 c. more cayenne
  pepper sauce

1 Tbs. mayonnaise

1 (12-oz.) can beer

2 c. cooked beans
  (cannelloni,
  great northern, pinto)

Garnish: blue cheese

DIRECTIONS

Marinate the chicken in 3 tablespoons of hot sauce overnight.

Melt the butter in a large skillet. Cut the chicken into half-inch cubes and dredge in the flour. Saute them until golden-brown in the butter.

Add the celery and continue to simmer for 2 or 3 more minutes.

Add the 1/2 cup of hot sauce, mayonnaise, beer and beans. Bring to a boil and then reduce to a simmer for 20 to 30 minutes. Ladle into bowls and sprinkle with crumbled blue cheese.

SERVING
4

NOTES
Your taste buds will think you're eating Buffalo wings, but there's none of the mess, and far less fat with this version. Use a nice crumbly blue cheese, and garnish each bowl with a celery stick.

SUBMITTED BY:
Chris Fennimore

A-Ole

INGREDIENTS

1 c. olive oil

15 cloves garlic, minced

1 small onion, chopped

2 cans flat anchovies, packed
   in oil

1 bunch fresh parsley,
   chopped, or 3 Tbs. dried

2 tsp. basil

1 tsp. black pepper

1 tsp. paprika

1 (14-oz.) can black pitted olives,
   chopped

Salt and pepper

Bay leaf

1 (12-oz) box fresh sliced
   mushrooms

About 2 lbs. pasta of your choice

1 lb. grated Locatelli
   romano cheese

DIRECTIONS

Heat oil in frying pan. Add garlic and onion, then anchovies and their oil. Mash anchovies until they liquefy, then add all herbs and spices. Mix thoroughly. Add olives and mushrooms, cover, and turn heat to low. Stir occasionally, adding more olive oil if needed.

Cook pasta, drain and mix with sauce. Add cheese (you can never put on too much cheese.) Enjoy.

SERVING
8

NOTES

This is not a recipe for the faint of heart. The spicy, salty, robust flavors of this dish jump out and grab you. Art told me to use a little more than 2 pounds of pasta because, as he says, "You never want to lay in short." Firefighters know what he means.

SUBMITTED BY:
Art Sallustio

Chicken and Dumplings

INGREDIENTS

6 c. water

1 (10³/4 oz.) can chicken broth

1 (10³/4 oz.) can cream of
   chicken soup

1 (10³/4 oz.) can cream
   of mushroom soup

1 tsp. garlic powder

1 medium onion, chopped

1 tsp. salt

1/2 tsp. pepper

2-3 lbs. boneless chicken,
   cut into bite-size pieces

2 (16-oz.) packages refrigerated
   biscuits or homemade
   dumplings

DIRECTIONS

Bring water, broth, soups and seasonings to a light boil.

Add chicken and return to the boil.

Add biscuits or dumplings and continue to boil, covered, until the
biscuits are done, in about 20 minutes.

SERVING
4-6

NOTES
There were so many good
cooks in Kevin's firehouse
that he couldn't get a
recipe in edgewise. When
he finally got his chance,
this was the dish he made.

SUBMITTED BY:
Kevin Jackson

Reuben Casserole

INGREDIENTS

1 (32-oz.) bag sauerkraut,
   very well-drained

1 lb. deli-style corned beef,
   chipped

1 (8 oz.) bottle Thousand
   Island dressing

1 lb. swiss cheese, sliced

12 slices of buttered rye bread,
   cut in 1-inch cubes

DIRECTIONS

Preheat oven to at 350°.

In the bottom of a 13x9x2-inch casserole, layer the sauerkraut, then the corned beef, dressing and swiss cheese.

Top with the buttered rye bread cubes.

Bake, uncovered, for 30 minutes.

Let cool slightly to set and it's ready to go.

SERVING
6

NOTES

This is like a giant reuben sandwich that serves six and can be eaten from a buffet dish. And think of the variations on other grilled sandwiches like rachels and monte cristos and even BLTs.

SUBMITTED BY:
Denean Y. Ross

Lentil Soup

INGREDIENTS

2 c. dried lentils

2 medium onions, sliced

2 carrots, chopped

2-3 ribs celery, chopped

2 small potatoes, diced

2-3 sprigs of parsley

1 bay leaf

7-8 c. chicken stock

Ground pepper to taste

DIRECTIONS

In a large pot, combine all ingredients.

Bring to a boil. Cover and simmer for 2 hours.

Add pepper to taste. Serve hot.

SERVING
6-8

NOTES
This is the kind of soup that is good for what ails you. As a matter of fact, it's good if nothing ails you at all, and it comes from one of our most loyal contributors: Catherine Monte Carlo.

SUBMITTED BY:
Catherine Monte Carlo

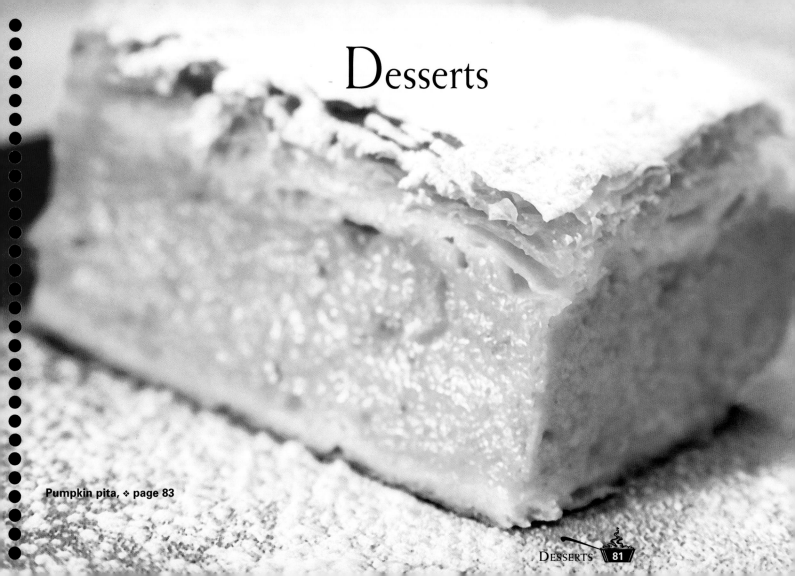

Desserts

Pumpkin pita, ❖ page 83

There's a wonderfully hedonistic saying that goes, "Life is uncertain. Eat dessert first."

Sometimes we measure the success of our cooking marathons by the number of recipes we receive. At other times, we measure the number of cookbooks that people request. Or we might look at the size of the audience that tuned in to see the show. But if we judged our programs by the number of blissful "oohs" and "aahs" heard during the tasting of the food, "'D' Is for Dessert" would be the clear winner. We had no trouble finding volunteers to answer the phone that day. Here are some of the best dessert and sweets recipes from that and other marathons over the years.

Pumpkin Pita (PUMPKIN SHEET PIE)

INGREDIENTS

1 qt. milk

1/2 c. cream of rice

2 c. sugar

2 Tbs. butter

1 15-oz. can pumpkin

4 beaten eggs

2 tsp. pumpkin pie spice

1 c. (2 sticks) butter, melted

1 lb. phyllo dough

DIRECTIONS

Cook the milk, cream of rice, sugar and 2 tablespoons of butter until thick, stirring constantly. Remove from heat and let cool slightly. Fold in the pumpkin, eggs and spice.

Preheat oven to 350°. In a 9x13-inch pan, layer a half-pound of phyllo, buttering each sheet well according to package directions. Pour pumpkin mixture over. Layer the other 1/2 pound of phyllo over, making sure to butter each sheet well. Score the top into 16 or 20 pieces. Bake for 1 hour, until the top is golden. Dust top with confectioners' sugar before serving.

SERVING
16

NOTES
If you've never used cream of rice before, you can find it in the hot cereal section of the supermarket near the cream of wheat and oatmeal.

SUBMITTED BY:
Pam Lagios

Eggnog Cheesecake

SERVING
10

NOTES

You could serve hot dogs and kraut for dinner, but if this is dessert, your guests will leave raving about your sumptuous meal. Applying the whipped cream with a pastry bag is the proper final touch on this memorable dessert.

SUBMITTED BY:
Chris Fennimore

INGREDIENTS

For the crust:

1 c. pecan halves

1 c. graham cracker crumbs

1/4 c. firmly packed brown sugar

5 Tbs. unsalted butter,
   melted and cooled to room
   temperature

For the filling:

2 lbs. (4 8-oz. pkgs.)
   cream cheese

1 c. sugar

3 Tbs. cognac, brandy or dark rum

2 tsp. vanilla extract

3/4 tsp. ground nutmeg

4 large eggs

Optional: powdered sugar,
whipped cream with nutmeg

DIRECTIONS

For the crust:

Preheat oven to 350°. Spread the pecans on a baking sheet and toast in oven for about 10 minutes. Let them cool. Leave oven at 350°. In a food processor fitted with a metal blade, combine the toasted pecans, graham cracker crumbs and brown sugar and process to grind finely. Add the melted butter and process until the crumbs begin to stick together. Press the crumbs into the bottom and up the sides of a 9-inch springform pan. Wrap aluminum foil around the outside of the pan and bake at 350° for about 10 minutes. Remove from the oven and allow to cool.

For the filling:

In the large bowl of an electric mixer, combine the cream cheese and sugar. Beat until well-blended, then add the cognac, brandy or rum, vanilla and nutmeg. Add the eggs one at a time, beating after each addition just until combined. Pour into the cooled crust. Bake about 1 hour, until the center still quivers slightly when the pan is shaken. Transfer to a rack and let cool. Cover with aluminum foil and refrigerate overnight or for up to 3 days. Run a knife around the pan sides to loosen the cake, remove the foil and release the pan sides. Decorate the top of the cake with powdered sugar or with a ring of whipped cream sprinkled with nutmeg.

Yogurt Pie

INGREDIENTS

2 c. crushed strawberries,
   raspberries or blueberries

1 (8-9 oz.) can sliced peaches
   or apricot halves, drained
   and mashed

1 (8-9 oz.) can crushed
   pineapple, drained

2 (8-oz.) containers plain
   Dannon yogurt

1 (8-9 oz.) pkg. Cool Whip

Graham cracker crust

Garnish: fresh fruit to match
   your choice of filling
   (optional)

DIRECTIONS

Combine crushed fruit and yogurt in bowl.

Fold in Cool Whip, blending well.

Spoon into crust and freeze 4 hours.

Remove and place in fridge for 30 minutes before serving.

Store leftovers in freezer.

SERVING
6

NOTES
Wouldn't it be nice to have
one of these in the freezer
for unexpected company?
Just make sure to seal it
well in a resealable bag.

SUBMITTED BY:
Nancy Polinsky

Berry Clafouti

INGREDIENTS

For the pastry:
4 slightly beaten egg whites
2 slightly beaten whole eggs
1/3 c. granulated sugar
3 Tbs. honey
2 Tbs. orange juice
1 tsp. vanilla
1 1/2 c. vanilla yogurt
1 c. all-purpose flour
1 c. each raspberries, blueberries and sliced strawberries
2 tsp. sifted powdered sugar

For the strawberry sauce:
1/4 c. sugar
1/8 tsp. salt (optional)
3 Tbs. cornstarch
1 c. water
1 3/4 c. frozen sliced sweetened strawberries, thawed

DIRECTIONS

For the pastry:

In a large bowl, beat together egg whites, eggs, granulated sugar, honey, orange juice and vanilla with a wire whisk or an electric mixer on low speed until light and frothy. Stir in yogurt until mixture is smooth. Add flour. Beat until combined and mixture is smooth.

Preheat oven to 375°. Coat a 10-inch one-piece quiche dish (not the kind with a removable bottom) with nonstick cooking spray. Arrange desired berries in bottom of dish. Pour batter over fruit. Bake 30-35 minutes or until center appears set when shaken. Cool on a wire rack for 30 minutes.

For the sauce:

Combine sugar, salt, water and cornstarch. Boil one minute. Add strawberries and heat until mixture is clear and thick. Also good on pancakes, waffles and ice cream.

Serve clagouti warm with strawberry sauce. Sprinkle with powdered sugar.

Each serving has: 200 calories and 2 grams total fat.

SERVING
6-8

NOTES
This low-fat dessert was one of the favorite recipes from our "'H' Is for Healthy" marathon. The strawberry sauce adds a few more calories, but still no fat.

SUBMITTED BY:
*Alice Valoski;
sauce by Carolyn Beinlich*

Peach Cobbler

INGREDIENTS

6 medium peaches

1/3 c. sugar

3/4 c. unbleached all-purpose
   flour

3/4 tsp. baking powder

Pinch salt

6 Tbs. nonfat milk

6 Tbs. liquid egg substitute

1/2 tsp. vanilla extract

DIRECTIONS

Preheat oven to 400°. Peel and slice peaches. You should have about 4 cups. Sprinkle with 2 teaspoons of sugar taken from the 1/3 cup. In a bowl, stir together remaining sugar, flour, baking powder and salt. In a larger bowl, whisk together milk, egg substitute and vanilla. Add dry ingredients to wet ingredients and stir just to blend. Batter will be thick.

Place peaches in a 9-inch nonstick pie pan. Spoon the batter over the peaches, smoothing it with the back of a spoon. It doesn't need to cover the peaches completely. In fact, it looks nice if some of the peaches are poking through. Bake until the peaches are bubbly and the topping is browned, about 30 minutes.

SERVING
8

NOTES
This simple, low-fat recipe really lets the flavor of fresh peaches come through.

SUBMITTED BY:
Nancy Polinsky

Each serving has: 110 calories, 1.8 grams of fat and 2.9 grams of protein.

Quick Coffee Cake

INGREDIENTS

1/2 c. vegetable oil

2 large eggs, beaten

1 c. milk

3 c. all-purpose flour

11/2 c. sugar

4 tsp. baking powder

1 tsp. salt

1/2 c. brown sugar, packed

1 Tbs. cinnamon

2 Tbs. melted butter

1/4-1/3 c. flour

DIRECTIONS

Butter a 9x13-inch pan. Preheat the oven to 375°. Mix together the oil, eggs and milk. Add the flour, sugar, baking powder and salt, and mix until just combined. Pour into prepared pan.

Mix brown sugar, cinnamon and melted butter.

Add enough flour to make a fairly dry crumble. Sprinkle over the top of the cake.

Bake for approximately 30 minutes or until cake springs back when lightly touched.

SERVING
8

NOTES

John Marthens told us he often made this cake when he was on the watch for night turns as a firefighter. The firehouse was filled with the aroma of the cinnamon topping gently browning in the oven.

SUBMITTED BY:
John Marthens

Blueberry-Streusel Muffins

INGREDIENTS

For the streusel topping:

1/4 c. cold butter, cut into 4 pieces
1/4 c. sugar
3/4 c. all-purpose flour
1 tsp. freshly grated lemon peel
1/2 tsp. ground cinnamon

For the muffins:

2 c. all-purpose flour
2 tsp. baking powder
1/2 tsp. baking soda
3/4 tsp. salt
1/3 c. sugar
1/2 tsp. ground cinnamon
1/4 tsp. ground nutmeg
2 tsp. freshly grated lemon peel
2 eggs, room temperature
1 (8-oz.) carton blueberry-flavored
   yogurt, room temperature
1/4 c. (1/2 stick) butter, melted
1/2 tsp. vanilla extract
1 1/4 c. fresh or frozen
   blueberries, not thawed

DIRECTIONS

For the topping:

Combine all ingredients in a medium bowl. Use a pastry blender or two knives to cut in butter until mixture resembles coarse crumbs. Set aside.

For the muffins:

Grease 18 muffin cups or line with paper liners.

Preheat oven to 400°.

In a large bowl, stir together flour, baking powder, baking soda, salt, sugar, cinnamon, nutmeg and lemon peel; set aside. In a medium bowl, lightly beat eggs. Stir in yogurt, butter and vanilla. Stir into flour mixture only until dry ingredients are moistened. Fold in blueberries until evenly distributed. Spoon batter into prepared muffin cups until half full. Sprinkle top of each muffin with about 2 rounded teaspoons of topping. Bake 15-20 minutes, or until a wooden pick inserted in center comes out clean. Serve hot.

SERVING

Makes 16-18 muffins

NOTES

There is something about the combination of nutmeg and lemon that accentuate the flavor of blueberries. This recipe actually goes together much more quickly than it might appear. Just make sure to have all your ingredients ready before you begin.

SUBMITTED BY:
Penny Lawrence

Apple Cake

INGREDIENTS

3 c. flour

1 1/4 c. oil

2 1/2 c. sugar

1 tsp. salt

1 tsp. baking soda

3 eggs

2 tsp. vanilla

2 tsp. cinnamon

Dash of ground cloves

3 c. diced apples

1-2 c. chopped pecans

DIRECTIONS

Preheat oven to 350°.

Mix ingredients by hand until just blended. Spoon into a 10-inch tube pan.

Bake for 1 1/2 hours.

SERVING
8-10

NOTES
This mix-dump-and-bake recipe has all the attributes of a Nancy Polinsky favorite: easy, no mess, absolutely delicious.

SUBMITTED BY:
Nancy Polinsky

Tarte Tatin

INGREDIENTS

For the filling:

4 lbs. apples, peeled, cored and
halved (any good cooking
apple will do)
2 Tbs. lemon juice
1/2 c. (1 stick). unsalted butter
1 1/2 c. sugar
3 Tbs. water

For the pastry:

1 c. flour
1 Tbs. sugar
6 Tbs. cold unsalted
butter, cubed
2 1/2 Tbs. ice water

DIRECTIONS

For the filling:

Preheat oven to 350°. Place apples into a bowl and toss with
lemon juice. Melt butter in an 8-inch cast-iron skillet. Stir in sugar
and water. Cook over medium heat until brown caramel forms—
about 8-10 minutes. Place apples tightly together in the skillet and
cook for 5-8 minutes. Place skillet into oven and bake for 25 minutes. Remove skillet from oven. Increase oven temperature to 425°.

For the pastry:

Place flour, sugar and butter into a food processor and process for
about 5 seconds to a cornmeal consistency. With the machine running,
slowly add water and process for about 10 seconds, until a ball of
dough forms. Roll into a 10-inch round and refrigerate for 10 minutes.

Cover skillet with pastry, tucking the edges along the inside of the
skillet. Make 4 slits in the pastry. Place skillet in the upper third of
the oven and bake for 25 minutes. Remove from oven and place on
rack to cool for 5 minutes.

Loosen crust from around sides of skillet with a knife. Place a dish
on top of the skillet and carefully invert tarte onto plate. Serve warm.

SERVING

6

NOTES

For this French
masterpiece, it helps to
have a well-seasoned
black skillet that goes
easily from stovetop to
oven. And don't bother
serving this unless you
have some French vanilla
ice cream to go along
with it.

SUBMITTED BY:
Jim Baran

Cashew Butter Toffee

INGREDIENTS

2 c. sugar

1 lb. (4 quarters) butter

1 lb. cashews

SERVING
Makes 2 pounds

NOTES
Make sure you dissolve
the sugar completely in
the butter, and let it boil
without disturbing,
or the butter may
separate. And please be
careful: The boiling toffee
is extremely hot.

SUBMITTED BY:
Chris Fennimore

DIRECTIONS

Butter a heavy jellyroll pan.

In a heavy 3-quart saucepan over moderate heat, dissolve the sugar in the butter and bring to a slow boil. Using a pastry brush and cold water, wipe down the sugar crystals that may have formed on the side of the pan. Allow the sugar and butter mixture to boil slowly until the mixture reaches 290° on a candy thermometer. **Do not stir during this time.**

Remove from heat, stir in the cashews and pour into prepared pan. Quickly, with the back of a wooden spoon, spread the mixture in the pan until it is as flat as possible. After about 5 minutes of cooling, score the toffee into squares so that it will be easier to break apart later. When the toffee is completely cool, break into pieces and store in an airtight container.

TJ Finger Cookies

INGREDIENTS

1 c. sugar

1 c. (2 sticks) butter

1 tsp. vanilla

About 80 salted crackers

12 oz. chocolate morsels

1 c. toasted chopped nuts

DIRECTIONS

In a heavy 3-quart saucepan, dissolve the sugar in the butter and bring to a boil. Cook for 2 minutes longer, then remove from the heat and add the vanilla.

While the sugar and butter are cooking, line a 10x15-inch jelly roll pan with aluminum foil and spray with nonstick spray. Completely cover the bottom of the pan with a layer of salted crackers. Preheat oven to 350°.

Carefully pour the butter/sugar mixture over the crackers, trying to moisten them all. Put into oven for 10 minutes.

Take the tray out of the oven, and sprinkle with the chocolate morsels. Wait a minute for the chocolate to soften, and then spread evenly with a spatula. Sprinkle with the chopped nuts and refrigerate until firm.

Remove from pan and peel away the aluminum foil. Break into pieces and store in an airtight container. (Or eat immediately!)

SERVING
Makes 6 dozen

NOTES
These cookies get their name from our young friend T.J. (Thomas) Herrle. He once burned his finger while making a batch of these with my wife, Laura. It's been 10 years, and she still feels guilty.

SUBMITTED BY:
Chris Fennimore

Acknowledgements

Many people helped to make this book possible. Many thanks go to Joe Certo for his help with the cooking and plating of the food for the photographs; Lilli Mosco, WQED vice president of membership and development; Jamie Ivanac, membership coordinator; Eric Brown and Patrick Neil, production artists; and John Seekings, director of promotions.

And once again, we thank Don's Appliance Sales & Service, Maggie's Building Solutions and KitchenAid for their contributions to the QED Kitchen. And special thanks to our advertising supporters in this book—Arhaus, Pittsburgh Brewing Co., Emerald Sales and Consumer Credit Counseling Service of Western Pennsylvania Inc.

Fiesta tableware courtesy of the Homer Laughlin China Co., Newell, W.Va., 800/452-4462 or www.hlchina.com

Page 9:
Stuffed cherry tomatoes and marinated mushrooms.
12 1/4-inch hostess tray, white; 5 5/8-inch small bowl, sea mist

Page 23:
Stuffed french toast and rolled omelette.
11-inch round serving tray on top of inverted rimmed soup bowl, both periwinkle; 7 1/4-inch salad plate, cinnabar

Page 37:
Hot sausage soup and sausage rolls.
9-inch rim soup bowl, rose; 11 3/4-inch chop plate, cinnabar; tripod bowl, yellow

Page 51:
Couscous, apricot and pistachio salad.
11 5/8-inch oval platter, cinnabar

Page 65:
Macaroni and cheese.
9 5/8-inch oval platter and napkin ring, turquoise

Page 73:
Buffalo chicken chili.
9-inch rim soup bowl and 9 1/2-inch relish/utility tray, juniper

Page 74:
A-ole.
13 5/8-inch oval platter, sea mist

Page 81:
Pumpkin pita.
7 1/4-inch inch salad plate, cinnabar

Recipe Contributors

The Success of our cooking shows has always been founded on the generosity of so many great cooks who generously send in their recipes to share. We've included some of the stand-out recipes from our past cooking marathons—and here are the folks responsible: ▼ ▼ ▼

Daniel K. Boyd,
O'Hara Township

Barbara Knezovich,
McKeesport

Susan Mihalo Van Riper,
Hampton Township

Jan Herrle,
Garfield

Alyson Sprague,
Sewickley

Barbara Knezovich,
McKeesport

Antoinette Jucha,
Scott Township

Horace Miles,
Mount Washington, and
Family Services

Pauline Lowery,
Mount Ararat Baptist
Church, East Liberty

Joe Fennimore,
New Paltz, N.Y.

Chuck Fennimore,
Durham, N.C.

Kevin Jackson,
Engine Co. No. 39,
Troy Hill

Art Sallustio,
Engine & Truck Co.
No. 4, uptown

Denean Y. Ross,
East Pittsburgh

Pam Lagios,
Holy Cross Greek
Orthodox Church,
Mount Lebanon

Catherine Monte Carlo,
Monongahela

Alice Valoski,
Women's Health
Initiative, University of
Pittsburgh Health
Studies Office, Oakland

John Marthens,
Highland Park,
No. 4 Engine & Truck Co.,
uptown

Roy Haley,
Sewickley

Greg Alauzen, chef,
The Steelhead Grill,
Marriott City Center,
uptown

Denise Robbins,
Greensburg

Marian Albert,
St. George Antiochian
Orthodox Church,
Oakland

Jim Baran has sent in

recipes for nearly all of the "QED Cooks" marathons and has been good enough to come on and demonstrate his love for cooking on many of the shows. Jim is a surgeon who lives in O'Hara Township with his wife, Carole, and their two children, Tracey and Laura. Although he's always been interested in cooking, he became more seriously involved after Carole enrolled him in some classes at the International Culinary Institute as a birthday present.

Nancy Polinsky has

been associated with WQED since 1986. She hosted the station's very first cooking marathon, in 1988, and since then has tasted hundreds of recipes in the QED kitchen, each one better than the last. She grew up in South Carolina, surrounded by a mother, father and sister who are wonderful cooks. However, she insists that she failed to inherit that particular talent and considers it a minor miracle when she gets a full meal on the table for her husband, WPXI-TV anchorman David Johnson, and their two boys, Michael and Eric.

Joe Certo is another

medical person who's just as comfortable in an apron at the stove as he is in his Penn Hills dentist's office. In addition to sending in recipes and appearing on several programs, Joe is often behind the scenes doing preparation work and washing dishes during our marathons—and for this edition of *The Best of QED Cooks*. It's really a family affair with the Certos: his wife, Alberta, has helped to type recipes for the cookbooks, while son Michael and daughter Christine have helped in the kitchen for several marathons.

Penny Lawrence

first came on our " 'B' Is for Berry" marathon with a recipe that used phyllo in a nonthreatening way. She's been sending in and demonstrating simple and delicious cooking techniques ever since. Penny's family owned the Blockhouse Cafe in downtown Pittsburgh for 44 years, so you might say that cooking is in her blood. You'll often see Penny's name as an instructor for cooking classes around town, and she also does catering. We're glad she still finds time for "QED Cooks."

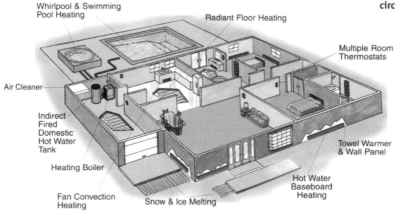

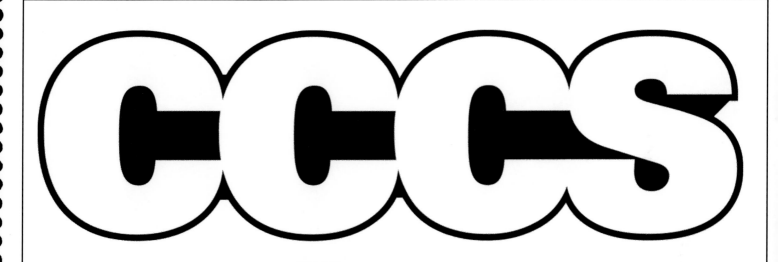

CONSUMER CREDIT COUNSELING SERVICE

FREE CONFIDENTIAL COUNSELING

412-390-1300

Index

numbers in italics are photos

Index

numbers in italics are photos